CHANGE TO TRUTH INTO REALITY

Written By:YAH'S Vessel

Introduction

This not your average book is to help you not hurt you. Real Truth! Historic you may say!

How I got into this knowledge when I start research on my own and find who I really am is not an African American but I'm an Hebrew Yisraelite or I can say Israelite, Black People today are The Chosen Children of THE MOST HIGH but only few will get this knowledge. We Not Africans,We Not Egyptians,We Not Muslims, We Hebrews And Israelites. We believe for so long that we are so equal with every others nations what the word call races,Now I would put scriptures in this,Because it time for The Blacks that's want to know this and has a ear. Did you know that you read Acts chapter for yourselves about church and if you have a bible book Read Acts chapter in the book in The New Testament but I love The Old Testament in the bible. Read The Book Of Jasher, The Book Of Enoch,The Book Of Jubilees,The Book Of The Apocrypha 1611 Edition,If you want to learn history of our forefathers who is Abraham,Isaac,Yakoov which in English Term Jacob.Let me tell you a little about myself I been knowing this knowledge of truth for almost 13 years now when I knew the secrets of America and propaganda they push.Now if my book don't sell it still getting told.We are THE MOST HIGH precious Jew and culture is like no other! Read Genesis chapter in another scripture in will of what prove in Genesis say and let get it And THE LORD formed man of the dust of the ground ,what color the dust on the ground Brown right or you can say Bronze so what we are today is so call Black and Brown Skinned continue and breathed into his nostrils the breath of life; means Human continue and man became a living soul,Still not convince Read Daniel chapter and Revelation chapter for yourselves.And it will tell you that how THE MOST HIGH'S BEGOTTEN SON LOOKS LIKE and it go get in details about THE MOST HIGH'S SON.This world is ran by Satan and his fallen angels offspring but THE MOST HIGH controls everything Read Isaiah chapter/ The Puppet Masters in this world is ran by The 3 Percent bankers of The Rothschild and The Rockefeller,The Bilderberg the main players are Evelyn De and Jacob Rothschild! They call them The 13 Bloodline Of illuminati but ILLUMINATI only means The Enlighten Ones but The Rothschild aren't the enlightening ones that are awoke,They(The Elites) are really call NWO (New World Order) Secret Society or Secret Societies,Well The Elites are The Rothschild,The Rockefeller,

The Bilderberg and The Synagogue Of Satan is The So Call Jews which they Khazar and Zionist They not The Real Jews that why they call themselves Jewish,We are The Real Jews Hebrew The So Call Black People today.And White People well so call White People today you are The Gentiles and you RESEARCH everything that I'm writing here. I knew about how this system works here in America, Education Yourselves Learning For Yourselves/ I knew how wicked people are on the regular basic. And spirits are real but most people don't see that and think you crazy.People today are like walking zombies and all they want to hear is how many entertainers are coming to town,the latest fashion,some stupid Jordan Shoes,what house they live in, I go own a house crap,we go get that pie in the sky,they want to be famous, I can go on and on but keeping it pushes,If you still not convince that THE BEGOTTEN SON is BRONZE read Daniel chapter\The truth is you in the matrix and program to believe that The Government is right for you but someone is in his pockets too. All President is selected and not elected. Now ok to keep focus of get this knowledge to the best of your ability.You know they give you these slave names because we broken The 614 OF THE LORD'S LAWS STATUTES AND COMMANDMENTS/.It not 10 COMMANDMENTS/It's 614 LAWS that THE LORD give to Moses for 40 Days and 40 Nights in Biblical Times.That what The Zionist=Fake Jews wanted you to believe that it only 10 they want to so call follow.And your passa=pastor at these churches has said The Laws Are Done Away with but according to THE MESSIAH said HE wasn't here to destroy the laws HE was to fulfilled THE LAWS STATUTES AND COMMANDMENTS.So that debunk what they talking about. Most Pastors and Bishops are Masons and apart of the 501(c) 3=Government Funded and meeting they don't have to pay no TAXES.Why still go to church? Why you still watch T.V.?Alot of you are Book Smart but don't have Common Sense. We were Spiritual Beings at one time. Like I was saying that this real truth ain't for everybody and it's really not it only for few of them. This planet is curse because why you think we as so call Black People are last of everything,Example every nations can tell us what to do don't they? Every nations knew who we really are but we don't know who we are is Hebrew.Alot of So Call Black People hate themselves and hate each other for no reason because they been programmed to believe that we are our own worst enemy when your slave master Willie Lynch put the fear in the heart to hate each other,be jealous of each other,envy each other and it still working like a charm in the modern day as Corporation Slaves because you are still SLAVES we are on our 3 strike and final straw why you think alot of craziness going on this planet. And you want to question THE MOST HIGH but we can't questioning THE MOST HIGH.People in your families die everyday the scripture speak on this.You realize they be showing us slave movies like The Old Roots,Goodbye Uncle Tom,and other slave movies don't they always show The Hebrews Slaves just always was so submitter to they slave masters and that's not all the way true because all The Hebrews didn't obey their slave masters and The Hebrews fought their slave masters back and kill the slave masters too.But they won't add that part.Now you'll might know about The Nat Turner Story/The So Call Haitians also fought The Slave Masters back and why you think they have so many slave movies? To see if you finga it out yet! A lot of you don't know that the job are own by some MOBS and wear suits and tides call Corporation America and Master Mason.You working around Masons at your jobs everyday without knowing it. Exodus tell you about this in scripture for yourselves. For you Gentiles so call White People you have NO HISTORY.Also you Khazar Turkish,Irish,Polish,Fake Jews don't have No History as well you stole our history and stole our identity of culture and call Jerusalem/Yerusalem also knows Yisrael your land which THE MOST HIGH curse that land call Yisrael because of The Heathrens that there but we still got some of our people still there in Yisrael.Now these so people don't have a soul in they body and demons are inside them. Like your favorite calebs,your politician,your mayor,your so call president,sports,People In General,The Elites,Etc.are all DEMONIC. Now the earth hasn't never been round earth has always been FLAT and the gravity is of water and let me pull the two scriptures in Zechariah chapter and Revelation chapter Now THE MOST HIGH AND THE BEGOTTEN SON doesn't love the world.HE love his chosen children in this world but HE doesn't love everybody of this world either. If you still believe that you have rights you still haven't finga it out. You think society is for you So Call Black People think again. So Call Society is suppose to be against because this not our rest.So why be like your oppressor?Some of you so call Black People are still on that Martin Luther King Jr. non-sense that Non-Violence since we came from slave ship on boats it was nothing but Violences in Ancient Babylon=So Call America because The Zionist ostrached it. Gentiles only own 40 percent of slaves so that tell you they didn't really have power like most people think! The Zionist Khazar=Fake Jews own 75 percent of SLAVES by doing a slave trade with The So Call Arabs and The So Call Africans trade The Hebrew Yisraelites or Israelites the way you understand but The So Call Africans was the last ones to make a deal with The Zionist with The Slave Trade. Now some of the so call Africans which they are Hamitic People or you can say Hamite are our people and our ancestors goes back too Shem and we Shemites/Shem is Noah's son on also Ham is Noah other son as well as Yapheth=Japheth.THE MOST HIGH told Abel 2,000 years ago that we go be in captivity for 400 years in Read Genesis chapter if you get a chances. When Abel kept pleased and kept pleased with THE MOST HIGH about saving at least 50,40,30,20 righteous people in Wicked Sodom and Gomorrah but the only Hebrew that THE MOST HIGH in Sodom and Gomorrah is

Abel Nephew Lot and Genesis chapter discuss this THE TWO AHCH ANGELS came to Lot in human forms and told Lot to hide get his wife and families to hide in the mountains but Lot's families was laughing it off and they didn't take it serious but THE MOST HIGH was about destroy Sodom with fire, so Lot's family stay where they at and just was Lot's immediate family as they ran and hide in the mountains THE MOST HIGH has put Sodom and Gomorrah with hell of fire and Lot's Wife hard headed self like most So Call Black Women today are stiffneck turn back as she say looking for her children and THE MOST HIGH turn her to a pillow of salt. As far as scriptures is concern is 70 percent Man Written and 35 percent in parables. Just only believe in THE MOST HIGH and you don't have to be a christians or a religion to believe in THE MOST HIGH for real. There no such thing is a Rapture ain't see no spirit go take you in the sky and THE MOST HIGH go rescue you.Because people got that Rapture crap from those camps on Youtube Video. Research everything I'm telling you here!Now if you have Facebook Page go to search and type YAH'S Vessel and it will pop up and he has very good information on there (Facebook). Learn your history and learn who you are. People are so afraid of Man so fear of Man.Man just some greedy and jealous beings only out for themselves.Woman are so rebellious and don't listen to reason. She think she's all that in a bag of chip and she should not be in position to teach the world and I know she might won't like this book but who cares. This for the ear openers and eye openers only need to get this real truth. THE MOST HIGH is totally angry with us and HIS SON is coming back in a fury.People are scare of what Satan go do but not afraid of what THE MOST HIGH will do for real.Our people are destroyed for a lack of knowledge because our people reject knowledge Hosea chapter saids it in the scripture.The bible is somewhat our history but been tamped with but it not The White Man Bible. Now you see is so important to research on your own. Because America don't want and need any So Call Black People to think and find things out for themselves.They want and need everyone to be dumbfounded.Did you know that Colleges is a waste of time to go too? You really think is about your degree?No it not about that because you go work minimum wage unless you join some Fraternity and Sorority team which was set by Aliester Crowley google him.But yeah The Frat Brotherhood is The Male Team and The Sororities Sisterhood is The Female Team.The Black Boule and The Black Caucus is apart this as well. So college is not the way unless you going for Nursing,Dentist,and Medical. Have you realize they throwing up they hand gesture in them colleges also they do this in Hollywood and The Police Academy as well. Now you research about the hand gestures don't take my word for it.All of this and they control by The Tax Payers and The Rothschilds The 3 percent bankers.So they control this continent not a country because we not living in a so call country.We got our people in the four quarters on the planet. We got some So Call African are our people which they Hamitic People or you can say Hamites.We concerned as Shemites and Igbo Tribes.We are THE STRONGEST NATION on this galaxy.THE MOST HIGH made us precious and that why we HIS FAVOR and also we are the most stiffneck=hardheaded people on this planet.

Our people (So Call Black People Hebrew) started a nation,build a nation,and The Father and Mother of all nations! So Call White People you never build anything we did,you can't make Black Babies,You named everything after you but sat on your butt to watch us do all the works as we build America and everything that's in it.America always living off the works of the slaves.America live off on the backbone of the slaves.America is named after some Italian name Amerigo Vespucci and Africa was name after another italian name Leo Africanus and that why you get the term African American. We not a color people that was set up by racist Zionism.They call us that in slavery,they call at first Negro or Nigger,then they call us Colored,then they call us Afro Americans,then they call us African Americans,then they call us Black,and now they call us African Americans/Black.Look at your Birth Certificate for example it go even say Color,Negro,or Black for real.How you think we got here and stuff?If you came on them slaveship as So Call Negro,So Call Colored,So Call Black,then your forefathers and foremothers and some of you was slaves on them boats.Most of the so call Africans not The Hebrews=So Call Negro flu on planes not boats. But alot of So Call African People think they are better than us! But they eat mud cake in Africa.

True enough that our ancestor flee to Africa but our lesture doesn't go back there yea we ran to Africa to hide from The Romans to capture us again but So Call African didn't trade in other so call Africans they trade in The So Call Negro which they The Yisraelites to the Zionist=So Call Jews which they the fake one and also The So Call Arabs People enslave us as well as The So Call Africans.Now alot of people go think that I'm writing my opinion but alot things that you can research for yourselves that I'm writing is facts and factual.We were a wealth people once a upon of a time but we lose our way because we didn't hearken to HIS LAWS STATUTES AND COMMANDMENTS and also THE MOST HIGH put The Hebrews in slavery not Satan and The So Call Jew nor So Call White People/Read Deuteronomy The Whole 28 chapter for yourselves in the bible.If some of you want to hear 100% TRUTH this is the book to read. The truth might offend you but it suppose to hurt you! What you might think I'm doing is trying to start something but long it Truth and Spirit in THE MOST HIGH EYES it all good. Love is LAWS STATUTES AND COMMANDMENTS and if you LOVE THE MOST HIGH like you'll say you do then keep and follow HIS LAWS to the best of your ability.The Laws are in Genesis,Exodus,Leviticus,Numbers,and Deuteronomy but mostly in Leviticus chapters.Show you in scriptures will give you 7 of them The first on Genesis=And I will make my covenant between me and thee,and will multiply thee exceedingly./Exodus chapter=And thou shalt shew thy son in that day,saying,This is done because of what which THE LORD did unto me when I came forth out of Egypt.\Exodus chapter=Thou shalt not commit adultery./Leviticus chapter Speak unto the children of Israel,saying,If a soul shall sin through ignorance against any of the commandments of THE LORD concerning things which ought not to be done,and shall do against any of them:/Leviticus chapter Thou shalt not uncover the nakedness of a woman and her daughter,neither shalt thou take her son's daughter,or daughter's daughter,to uncover her nakedness; for they are her near kinswomen: it is wickedness./Number chapter=At the commandment of THE LORD they rested in the tents,and at the commandment of THE LORD they journeyed: they kept the charge of THE LORD by the hand of Moses. Deuteronomy chapter=The woman shall not wear that which pertaineth unto a man,meaning Women wearing jeans and pants that Men originally wear pants and jeans

continue neither shall a man put on a woman's garment: mean Men shouldn't put on a woman's dresses and skirts continue for all that do so are abomination unto THE LORD thy YAH. Now don't get it twisted it 614 LAWS STATUTES AND COMMANDMENTS not 10 commandments The Khazar=So Call Jews=Jew-ish People took 614 out it just put 10 commandments they only wanted to follow. We have good people in this world and we have bad people in this world.People told you that the world was go end so many time until THE MOST HIGH says it over people go use scare tactics. So it not 10 commandments it 614 Laws Statutes And Commandments. Now you wonder why these Zionist and Khazar call themselves Jewish mean doesn't contain too so they not Jews we as so call Black People are THE MOST HIGH THE LORD precious Jew.You can also research about 614 LAWS and who THE LORD chosen children is! You been in a big lie all of your lives and allot of you are comfortable in living a lie than to hear truth for real.The truth hurts most folks and they can't handle truth! And a lot of you have Book Sense but not Common Sense but few of you have Common Sense! This world is corrupt because we cost it,and we not save by grace we save by mercy and that Christianity Talk and because THE MOST HIGH has mercy of whom HE has mercy on and has compassion

on whom HE has compassion for that in Romans chapter So you'll that go too church need to ask your Pastors to read this scripture for yourselves,Your passa are deceiving and pimping you into tithe 10 percent of your money,your check,to the wolf in sheep clothed your Passa. Your passa ain't THE LORD'S SON. And The Pope every soul in the world that praise him as THE

MOST HIGH and a pedophile and you see how this world is corrupt and so demonic crazy. Our culture are very not just precious but very family oriented,very Brotherly and Sisterly Love,good business people,good family people,good visionary,strong,powerful,stick together,very spiritual,spiritual being,praying folks,and so upright,so righteous,and THE MOST HIGH shine down on them at the time but it few HE shining on today.In this generation is no role model,there no daddy finga,no communication, most women are retard,people are so obsess with they pets,they always saying enjoy your life,and the main thing they say I LOVE YOU! THE MOST HIGH is so nigh. THE BEGOTTEN SON will return. THE AHCH ANGELS are protecting the righteous and chosen for THE MOST HIGH.The people with good intention with children you need teach at a early age about THE MOST HIGH and about the reality of life in this world.Teach them

how to protect themselves in self-defense and go practice defending yourselves because you go need too.To be aware around be your surroundings of what type spirit people has and you walking in the valley of death everyday. Judgment is in this kingdom for real. Why you praising for riches and not do nothing but make poor decision on having it.Seem like the average person only pray to THE MOST HIGH when things go bad for them but forget THE MOST HIGH when good things happen for them.To serve THE MOST HIGH it will a long hard road HE take you left first then right. You got people believe in Religion,You got people believe in Christianity,You got people believe in Jehovah Witness,You got people believe in Buddha,You got people believe in Hindu,You got people believe in Wood and Stone,You got people believe in Judaism,You got people believe in Lucifer himself! All of these things really of Satanism. None of belief always believe they superior to one another and always arguing about something. Too much discrimination in this nation and so much critizism in this nation but only THE MOST HIGH that can control the nations. THE MOST HIGH won't save all people only HIS ⅓ and 144,000.THE MOST HIGH allow lot of things to happen this because it prophecy.

THE MOST HIGH loves those who love HIM and read that Proverbs chapter!When you praise THE MOST HIGH and give HIM glory HE show you stuff that you never imagine.The thing is are you ready to changes your lives,mature yourselves,respect yourselves,keep and follow THE MOST HIGH'S LAWS to the best of our ability,and keep the covenant.Too have this knowledge read what comes to mine.Search Truth and seek knowledge /Alot of people think consciously but they don't think spiritually.People that thinks it conscious not spiritual.Watch who you advice to your house because people feed demons in your homes.I'm not writing this book to even wake the whole world up nor I'm not to try to reach everybody neither. Matthew chapter said many were call but only few are chosen. And that's the truth! Encourage any one that need be a right path of direction of righteousness to THE MOST HIGH.Encourage few stand up,Encourage few to wake up,Encourage few to mature now, Encourage few keep THE MOST HIGH first,Encourage few to believe in THE BEGOTTEN SON,Encourage few to fast,And Encourage few to have Common Sense. A lot people contradict themselves of these pastors, preachers,deacons,

cardinals,bishops, evangelist, telvangelist, and minsties etc. all say one thing but does the opposite of what they say. 85 percent lies and 15 percent truth. Judaism worship Lucifer to the fullest! People love to say praise THE LORD but when it time to be about the word of THE LORD then go run to the so call White Man and these phat pastors at churches for a blessing. They don't tell you about seafood,pork,and GMO Food in Leviticus chapter and don't tell about being a just a just weight in Deuteronomy chapter.Moving on right now people need stop falling for illusion everything that you think you should have like finance for example THE MOST HIGH don't bless us with a lot of of finance=money,with a nice car,a big house,a big booty whore and people don't realize that Lucifer blesses too. And Lucifer=Satan is blessing these people with riches and materialism not THE LORD=THE MOST HIGH.THE LORD give you enough to survive and you will have to work for it with THE MOST HIGH for real! And THE MOST HIGH is a jealous MOST HIGH and HE takes on our jealousy when people talk bad about us when we has this much knowledge.Why you think we hated without a cost? We royalty! Nobody can't stand us,every nations want to steal our culture and be like us,sound like us,and now dress like us. But we allow them to do so and can't get too

mad at them. It not who better than the other nor you has the most money. Where the respect? Where the standard? Where the morals? I'm tell why we don't have these things anymore because we want to like our oppressor and want to be but Hebrew for real! People loves to compete with one another and business especially Corp America loves and having competition at their jobs and families and friends love to compete with one another and it ridiculous. Not too many stand up men no more,Not too many real men out there no more and if looking for stand up men T.V. they are nothing but coons and sellouts.Television is full of lies and give you nothing but garbage and bunch of subliminal stuff so your kids can wild out and adult dream big. Live your life accordly but don't live for the world. People hate truth but love lies! Like a trend one person do something everybody else follow alone with it. Live how THE MOST HIGH wants us to live like not man wants us to live in luxury. I know nobody perfect including myself accept THE MOST HIGH AND HIS SON. Our forefather did for the nations before our generation like Enoch,Noah,Shem,Abel,Issac,Jacob,Moses,Solomon,Peter,Paul,and James accomplish with The Yisraelites or you can just say The Hebrews.Paul was not a Christian of how Christians protray it! One minute these Roman Catholic Priest said Paul was a christian and they also lie about Paul said

The laws are done away with and that was irrelevant and untrue Paul never said THE LAWS are done away he said follow THE LAWS to the best of your ability and eat food of THE BEGOTTEN SON told us to eat and not to eat and partake in the word of THE MOST HIGH .Paul was a Hebrew by the way! Also Paul was a killer and THE BEGOTTEN SON still forgive him. All our forefathers had to recondition themselves to serve THE LORD.And THE AHCH ANGELS even help some of well spoken forefathers and appear to them. Because they always was in spirit. Alot of people never wanted too talk about Solomon David's son,because he was one our forefathers too. Solomon was a great man not just because he had over thousand wives because he give land away and Solomon that is only ask THE MOST HIGH for wisdom and knowledge and THE MOST HIGH give him wisdom and knowledge not only that he also give him riches too and Solomon never ask for riches either. The problem with Solomon was not only he was in love with them concubines but he started drawing and worship these concubines Gods which the six point star=Molech and THE MOST HIGH ridicule Solomon for practicing Molech and Solomon

heart turn on THE MOST HIGH because he was in love with them conibunes and THE MOST HIGH loved Solomon dearly but THE MOST HIGH had to take Solomon down. Now Nehemiah kill alot of Yisraelites that wasn't following THE LAWS STATUTES AND COMMANDMENTS that THE MOST HIGH wanted them to follow and we suppose to follow the Laws they should of follow and keep. Even THE MOST HIGH kill like 20,000 Yisraelites because they kept complaining,they kept messing with strange flesh,they kept worshiping wood and stone Gods,they kept complaining about meat and THE MOST HIGH has The Hebrews in the wilderness for 40 years that in Exodus and Numbers chapters and THE MOST HIGH heard Moses and HE got tired of The Hebrews complaining and heard they cry and gave them meat and they died off into eating so much meat THE MOST HIGH had to take them out.You also can research this. All these things happen in Biblical Times.And it stand today!These men the camps on Youtube talking about they the modern day David,oh they modern day Paul,they the modern day Peter and they

just some greedy phat pigs. Don't listen to there evangelist talk about prosperity just another way of getting your money. Pimps and pimpettes.TD Jakes is a pimp in a suit,Creflo Dollar is a pimp in a suit,Creflo said we don't have to follow THE LAWS STATUTES AND COMMANDMENTS anymore which THE MOST HIGH'S LAWS still stand today.Jamal Bryant is a pimp in a suit and Bryant said These Hoes Ain't Loyal but love those hoes.Joyce Meyer is a pimpette in a suit and she said THE LORD bless her to be a teacher and THE LORD didn't put the spirit on you Joyce and the rest of you women to teach in the pulpit. Read 1 Timothy chapter for yourselves. Stop lying and bear false witness on THE LORD like that. Juanita Bryum is a pimpette with a congregation for a foundation.Kenneth Copeland is the riches pimp in the 501(c) 3 church in a suit and Copeland said THE LORD spoke to him about getting a private jet./Insane

He also said Adam wasn't bless because he didn't tithe which wasn't no such thing in tithing in Adam's Time and you'll faithfully watch these

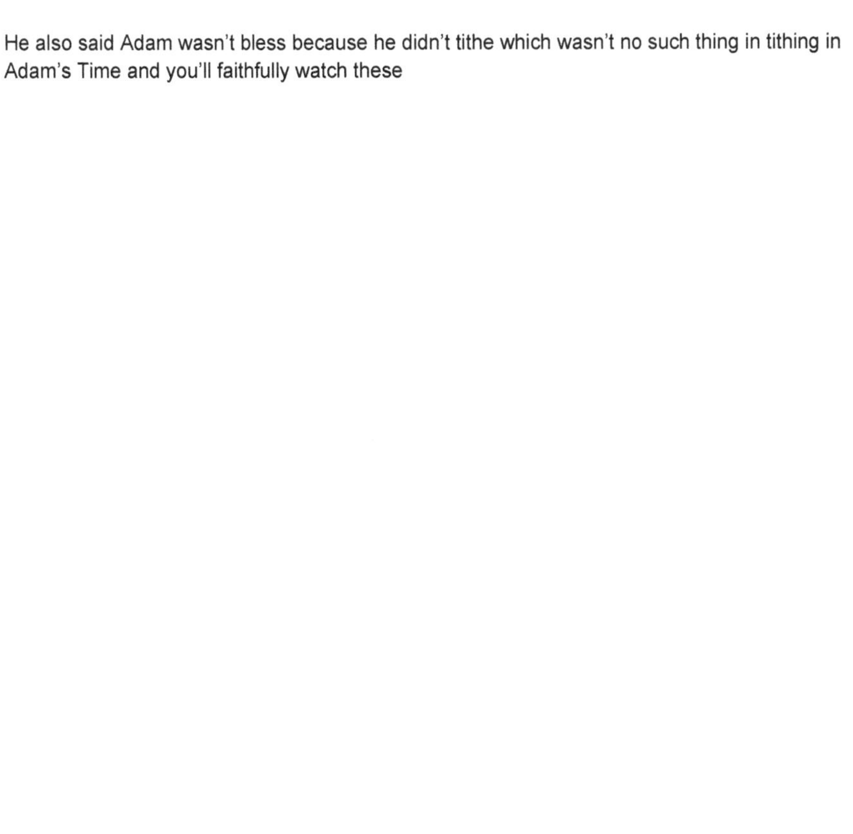

devils on T.V./ Benny Hinn is a Kambaal Worshiper and a pimp in a suit. Hinn try to play like he THE MOST HIGH'S SON trying to heal people with his hands,slapping his congregation,and thinking they heal and still in the hospitals and still sick. You have to pay the ultimate price for mocking THE MOST HIGH Benny Hinn. Frederick Price is a little pimp in a suit. Donnie Mcclurkin is a pimp in a suit.And Mcclurkin is gay like most pastors are.Even they So Call White People and So Call Black People even they gay,homosexual,or bi-sexual.Eric Robinson and Pat Robertson the devils themselves in a suit. Joel Osteen is a pimp in a suit teaching you prosperity with his fake smile. Johnny Dubon and Bishop Wayne T are pimps in a suit and Wayne T calling himself an Apostle and the Apostle was Paul in Biblical Times and it hasn't been an Apostle since then. Change the subject now All president is selected and not elected from George Washington,John Adams,Thomas Jefferson,James Madison,Jason Monroe,John Quincy Adams,Andrew Jackson, Martin Van Buren,William Henry Harrison,John Tyler,James

K.Polk,Zachary Taylor,Millard Fillmore,Franklin Pierce,James Buchanan,Abraham Lincoln,Andrew Johnson,Ulysses S. Grant,Rutherford B. Hayes,James A Garfield,Chester A. Arthur,Grover Cleveland,Benjamin Harrison,William Mckinley,Theodore Roosevelt,William Howard Taft,Woodrow Wilson,Warren G. Harding,Calvin Coolidge,Herbert Hoover,Franklin D.Roosevelt,

Harry S. Truman,Dwight D. Eisenhower,John F. Kennedy,Lyndon B. Johnson,Richard Nixon, Gerald Ford, Jimmy Carter,Ronald Wilson Reagan, George H.W. Bush,Bill Clinton, George W.Bush,Barack Hussein Obama,til Donald Trump all was selected by The Elites and they all White Masons. They all talk the same game and the game remain the same.None of these so call President had no control over this so call country because they was been controlled and puppets for Secret Societies The Elites.Just like they control houses,they control tax payers, and tax payers has said so also, they control the music industry,the colleges,the shelters,the gas station,etc. George Bush's Wife Barbara Bush is the daughter of Aleister Crowley.Satan

Worshiper himself when he was alive.75 percent of films are telling of what about to go down in real life! You'll look at movies for just entertainment.Don't it seem like when you speak truth seem like nobody hearing you for real. It seem like it come one ear out the other! No Black Man won't own anything in America unless The Zionist has control over it. Long you So Call Black in this country you will not own anything here. So Call Black People you need to get your mind off trying to own.Just do the best you can to survive. Is not about being rich and coming up. Just have enough for you

and your families immediate family. Survivor is the key not the money. Is ok to have money but don't let the money make you! Don't love the money either! To get your life together by stop eating pork,clean your temple,eat healthy to the best way you can,keep the laws to the best of your ability,and practice self defense. The deeper you get this knowledge the more you connected to your spirit.Now can you imagine if you connected to your spirit.Now can you imagine tune in your spirit you will clear some thoughts for real! So in 2 Timothy saids study thyself that be approve! 1 Peter said study your pure minds. We are living in the last days. Stuff is happening so fast we can't keep up on it. People so caught up of everybody is living like but themselves. So caught up in people business and mess.What can you do for yourselves? You need to ask yourselves that question! It seem they got you coming and going for real.Time is nigh! Hold study of what you know and you don't know! Because everybody doesn't want and need to hear this.People always want something but don't search for nothing they need.About

90% of people in America so call America follow trends.Like one person does things everyone seem to follow. We have more followers than leaders today like we did in the 50's and 60's followers well stool pigeon hardly no so call Black Leaders.

Page 26

I'm not an angry person that in some type of cult or camp. I'm not a religion Man Made,I'm not a christian Man Made,I'm not a Jehovah Witness Man Made,I'm not a Judea Man Made,I'm not teach or preach hate,I'm not an Atheist Man Made,I'm not a Scientist Man Made,I'm not an Egyptian Man Made,I'm not a Kemet nor Nubian Man Made, I'm not a Muslim Man Made, I only believe in THE MOST HIGH YAH OR YOU CAN SAY THE LORD AND HIS SON. I'm spiritual and righteous Brother. Our roots of hair of braids,locks,afros,breads,and natural hair that what we had in Biblical Times.And every nation in the world copying our style of roots but with straight hair. I don't see why our women The So Call Black Women still rocking the weaves and wigs then it have to be blonde too. I'm tell you this book might hurt some feelings.We need to go back to our original roots and stop trying so hard to look like our oppressor. Our melanin can last in the sun and it beautiful,it precious,it amazing,and our nature from generation after generation after generation. Our culture suffer the most but we will rise again and get things straight! Every nations had taken and stolen our culture and use it and use it today. Some of you might think it a conspiracy theory book but it not! It to help you not hurt you.

If you get offended by this book then it you! Some of you may can handle the truth and most of you can't handle the truth of reality.All prophets of THE MOST HIGH were Hebrews not Gentiles the so call White People which they Gentiles not Hebrews So Call Black People is and are The Hebrew Yisraelites. If you still think you So Call African then prove it! If you know THE BEGOTTEN SON is Black and I'm talking to you so call White People then have a Black Messiah on your pictures and walls.But you Gentile can't accept that and that name you call Jesus Christ is actually Caesare Borgia. It just research I do so don't take it personal.Seem like almost nobody don't want to serve THE MOST HIGH.They act like they do but most of them don't. About at least 75 percent of So Call Black Men that are lock up in jail and prison are innocent and you can research on your own. And the other 15 percent are guilty of the crimes.Moses was in jail in Biblical Times,Daniel was in jail in Biblical Times, Paul was in jail in Biblical Times,and Simeon Peter was in jail in Biblical Times. It wasn't call jail and prison then it was just call the cave.Paul was a killer before THE MOST HIGH chose him. Enoch was the only Hebrew Man that never taste death. People are afraid

Page 28

of the saying death but anyway step out of your comfort zone and think. I'm not trying to wake the whole world up but only few. THE MOST HIGH AND HIS SON is not of this world and if you know they persecute us just know they persecute THE MOST HIGH SON FIRST. And that in John chapter by the way! LORD means Master look it up. THE MOST HIGH brang us on this planet to be leaders and most people to busy been followers for real and that's the real truth!And in Romans chapter said what if some don't believe? You got to ask yourselves that! You won't get all of your answers in a book.You won't get all of answers in my book.Be careful of who you associate with, You have no friends well so call friend these days,But not trying to be your daddy or anything like that.When you become a man when you leave your daddy and mother house. Peter left his family home which it was a tent by the way.Yoseph=Joseph left his family home,Yacoov=Jacob left his family home,Abel left his family home and one of the richest man in the land not money,Solomon left The Hose Of Dawid=David and was rich and had over 1,000 wives and Solomon only wanted knowledge and THE MOST HIGH give him (Solomon) riches in land and shakurer=money silver and gold,All our forefathers had multiple wives. THE MOST HIGH never condemn a man for being with more than one woman.We give land for the children,We give clothing,we give food,we give shelter,and shared.You got to be real about THE MOST HIGH,You got to be serious about THE MOST HIGH,You got to know THE MOST HIGH on your own.I can't send you'll too the promise land or can't give you salvation only THE MOST HIGH SON can give you'll salvation. People take THE MOST HIGH as a joke but afraid of what Lucifer want you react but THE MOST HIGH will have you wait then HE will take action. But you have too acknowledge HIS ONLY BEGOTTEN SON.Knowledge isn't just power it's wealth not money wealth.Health is the wealth! The average person don't take anything serious until it happen. You take those individual serious for real. Focus on things that matters. Get your minds out the gutter! Everything that we going through we been through it and fought it before and I'm leave it at that.Things are getting crazier and crazier everyday. The evil spirits is among us and good spirits is among us. We walking in the valley of death everyday for real and that's in Psalms and Proverbs chapter I believe. If you have an immediate family take care of your families. Do what's best of you.When you unlearned and taught a certain way then when you find out things for yourself you stop following trends. Majority of individual will rather hear what their pastors say, what their deacons say, then what THE MOST HIGH say but I don't care of they period they are not THE MOST HIGH. I need to call out The Pope how these Catholic claim you a christian but molest children which it pedophila\pedophile and that's a cover up to call themselves christian so you wouldn't attack them so you wouldn't criticize them. A lot of people don't know why they calling themselves christians especially So Call Black People. Look it up the real truth behind it! The Pope is not THE MOST HIGH and he had some of his hands in slavery as well! Alot of jobs of brotherhood! Alot families are Masons and Freemasons especially so call White Families! Alot of individual are bamboolze. Being real is hard to gravity to most folks. Being fake is the new way of life now. Alot of hypocrites In this world full of evilness.You gotta take the bad with the good and the good with the bad! Sometimes it doesn't work. Individual want to be your buddy when you lie to them but don't won't anything to do with you,when you write,type,or speak truth. Truth hurts like a mug. Lies will prevail because every man and every woman is a liar,And so call White People can't stand when you call them the biggest lairs. When they say and always show so call Black People killing each other is mostly propaganda and fake news and which CNN,FOX News,ABC,CBS, New York Times,etc. tell you'll nothing but fake mess.Statacis shows more so call White People killing and raping each other more than so call Mexican People and so call Black People combine together.So Call White People doing most of the killing and that including crooked white cops as well,Research this too for yourselves,So Call White People are the number one murderers, number one rapist,number one on government assistance like food stamps government assistance, section 8 government assistance,government property government assistance,corp jobs government assistance,anything that had to do with govenor it's government assistance and corporation own. Here come So Call Mexicans now are number two thing with raping and killing each other and they raping other nations and culture beside themselves plus they the second on statasic that on Food Stamps then the So Call Black People are third on Food Stamps,Government Assistance, Murdering, Raping,etc. This what statistic shows but I thought we as So Call Black People are number one are doing everything in so call society because we have no society and we suppose to be doing all the killing and raping if we are only 13 percent of the population! I'm tell you why it only 13 percent because most of The So Call Black Men at least 75 percent of The So Call Black Men are lock up in prison and jail,75 percent of The So Call Black Women are Single Baby Mammas,Alot of So Call Black Men are dead, so you only have Black Women that's doing more of the killing that's your 13 percent because only at least 2 percent of Black Men killing and raping. Women out numbered

Men 10 til 1. So there's not enough Men to go around killing especially so call Black Men! But so call White Men are known for killing,molesting, and being raptist. On T.V. they want you so focus on So Call Black Men that doing all the crimes but it to distract you of what they doing behind the scenes. But White On White Crimes are worst than Black On Black Crimes and you know what the haters and nay slayers will say and react to reality! They want to throw stuff So Call White People do under the rug and they try to make you forget that they ancestor White People the evil ones how they took,rape,rob,and kill to change history with the help of The Fake Jews and Jobs chapter said the earth was giving to the hands of the wicked and they cover the faces there of, which is us Hebrews and they took and stole our identity and said they build everything they all sat on they butts and watch us build everything with THE MOST HIGH help.They will take what you start and build and capitalize it again us.They been doing from generation til generation after generation. I see some individual trying change history to get self-glory! You can't changes something that already happen and it come to pass. Plus it nothing new under the sun and it manifesting itself.

Please a reminded of who we are as a whole we are buildings, we inventory,we royalty,we started it and we will finish it. People don't have doubts in THE MOST HIGH and don't ever have doubts in THE MOST HIGH. Two of The 12 Disciples doubted THE BEGOTTEN SON and Simon Peter denied THE BEGOTTEN SON thrice means in Hebrew 3 Times. THE BEGOTTEN SON is real. THE BEGOTTEN SON will recompense the world and this really why HE doesn't love the world. I don't love the world nor the abominations of this world,100 percent corrupting of the world, people of the world with demonic and disturb spirits. 2 Timothy said study shew thyself approval again the chapter of this. THE MOST HIGH will not be denied. I know this will hurt feelings but it suppose too! I can't be soft this not a christian book. It for some to understand and this is not my truth it's THE MOST HIGH truth and words! Things will come and you wouldn't accept it of how it should be! People will hold on to stuff that not worth it.We were punish here in America to learn a lesson. Because we don't get favor of anything! No scholar won't tell it like it is, no pastor, no bishop, no preacher, no revenue,no ministriny, no deacon won't tell it like it is, your families won't tell it like it is, no so call White Man won't tell it like it is, They throw stuff in your face that the average person want to hear like Hollywood is the prime example of people want to see which it a bunch of nothing and our people love to hear and see of bunch of crap. They didn't want to tell the whole truth of slavery and what makes you think they go tell you 100 percent truth on anything? Ask yourself that! The more too this book is too learn,listen,and live your life to the best of your ability like THE BEGOTTEN SON who died for our sake. How come people on Facebook got more of the truth then the average Pastors does. I already call out some of the names earlier go back to page 22 til 23! Again The Hebrews are so called Negro,The Gentiles are so called White,Moabites are so called Chinese,Ammonites are so called Japanese, Cushites of Mesoptamia are so called Ethopians,The So Called Egyptians Mizraim= The Sudanese,Watusis,and Zulus,Canaanites=So Called South Africans,Midianites are so called Arabs,Philistines are so called Africans,Assyrians are so called Kuros,Babylonians are also so called Ethopians,Persian/Medes are so called East Indians,Greeks are also so called White

People, Romans are so called Edomites so called also White People,The Hamites are so called Africans as well, And The Ishmaelites are also so called Arabs. So your nationally doesn't have anything do with a color! The Zionist the so called Fake Jews made it about races not THE MOST HIGH HIMSELF. The J letter only been existed for 300 some odd years ago same time The Zionist took over America so call. And America also push color on you, push races on you which you not Black,you not White,You not Asian,You not Mexican, You not nothing what American protrayal that you are. If that the cases then why history repeating itself? If that the cases why the same people were back in Biblical Times are the same people that here today only differents they just call you Black,White,Asian,Arab,Mexican,and so on.Daniel was the last Hebrew Prophet THE MOST HIGH chosen. People hates truth and love lies! This is not bout me at all it's about real truth. People wants to changes history so bad not just The Power That Be it people that think they know it all and know everything supposedly. THE MOST HIGH won't let it happen at all. Changes history all you want! Don't believe the hype still that a woman is equal to a man which she's not and don't believe in any of the books in the bible that there was prophetless which Man is presume it The Khazar did this is because THE MOST HIGH never put a woman in front of the people in Biblical Times to teach a soul and women in the pulpit wish they shouldn't be in the frontline to begin with took it upon themselves to teach and preach like the man and always trying to challenge Men on every level. Everything we do women want to follow behind and do it. If THE MOST HIGH had you doing these thing The Man does that read Ecclesiastes and Ezekiel to find out.Our women are totally gone. Other nations of women submitts majority of them not all of them.Ladies if you got husbands learn from him at home. Women don't get is I'm talking about Shebrew Woman doesn't realize that she magnificent and unique but she want to be like so call White Women,she try to dress like her oppressor,she act like her oppressor,and she even talk like her oppressor. She even try to smell like her oppressor and even wear blonde fake hair to impress they oppressor. DNA really mean Does Not Acknowledge don't mean that you 1 Percent Asian,20 Percent Native Indians,70 Percent Black, 10 Percent White, You not Cherokee by the way and DNA is just a piece of paper and it does lies. You ain't no all type of texture don't fall for that non-sense.I'm not the first to say this and I'm not the last to say this. So keep focus,don't fall for anything,fear only THE MOST HIGH, You see the things that you desire ain't always the things you need! Don't waist your time on telling everybody you talk too the truth, real truth not just any truth! When you look at things spiritual and alot of things are spiritual! To stay positive you got to stay away from negative energy,so call friends, and so call families. Positive Mind Negative Energy/ And it say talking is cheap but when expose things and bad it up real truth and hardcore facts and it stings a bit you can't denied it! THE MOST HIGH will give you 100 folds if I or any other true brothers out there that doing the work to the end. The adversary will get recompense 10 fold. THE BEGOTTEN

SON is coming back in fury of vengeance and anger. Got to bring up Christianity got to expose this false doctrine by The Zionist and Christian Roman Catholic. First off I don't say for real Christ,Gospel,Christians,Christianity, Jesus,Cross,Church,God,and Bible I won't go into detail on that research them word for yourselves,In Greek they call non-believers Christians,Christos,or Christianos just mean poor fella in Aramic Manuscripts as well, Plus this in BCE Time this guy named Diety Serapis and his followers of Serapis was called Christianos which mean again poor fella! It just another pagan tradition and pagan worshippers of Diety Serapis that called themselves Christians and Christianos. But in Hebrew it called Mashiyach. Also at the Vatican Museum it call Pagan Christos Mithras. Like I just mention in Hebrew THE BEGOTTEN SON was and is Mashiyach and The 12 Disciples was Mashach. So the question is why do call Christianity which the worst thing happen since 325 A.D. of the The Council Of Nicaea and was a friend of Emperor Constantine who rule them all was Caesar. Also was involve was The Scribe and

Pharissee. If you wasn't following they philosphy you were slew mean kill. THE BEGOTTEN SON was against the Scribe and the pharissee philosphy and then on the third day when THE MASHIYACH and that exploring came on Rome forever and only thing that in Rome is dirt I believe and a piece left of the palace of Rome. And So Called White People these were your people that was cruflix THE BEGOTTEN SON.And So Called Arabs Mohammad wasn't no prophet and he couldn't read nor write. And religion isn't good to follow either.All religion does is philosphy alot. If you offended once again than it you! So Called Chinese People your Buddha is witchcraft! So called Indian your Hindu is witchcraft! My book wasn't trying to preach but too spread facts,tell real truth, and get the knowledge. Hope you support this and read it careful, This too heal you,encourage you, strengthen you, too shed light,educational,love,not a storyteller book it a reality check book,might be interested, might standout, might awakening you, it too help you,and spiritual.

Let's talk about Pagan Holidays now like your New Years Eve,New Years Day, Valentine Day,President Day,Groundhog Day,St.Patrick Day,April Fools,Easter Day,May Day,Mother Day,Memorial Day,Father Day,4th Of July,Labor Day,Columbus Day,Halloween Day,Veteran Day,Thanksgiving Day, Christmas Eve,and Christmas Day are all Pagan Holidays and Pagan Tradition by Romans their your people so call White People. New Years Eve and New Days stands for a new ritual, Valentine Day St Massacre is a bloody ritual for the Romans, President Day and Groundhog Day was added by The Elites, it a disaster day and so as April Fools by The Khazar another ritual day,St.Patrick Day the Satan Worshippers in green,Easter is Lent a sex symbol of Nimrod and Semartians but they throw you off with a Bunny Rabbit that hatch eggs and tell you that who the world ignorant call Jesus which HE really call YAHWEH BEN YAHWEH who resurrected on Easter but not true HE resurrected on the 3rd Day after The Passover meal nobody including myself know that day that he resurrected.May Day they added in the calendars like the rest was added,

Mother Day is Pagan Mother Day also Mother God,Mother Earth,and Mother Nature is all Roman Mythology,Memorial Day is another ritual day they added,Father Day is the Roman Gods Day,4th Of July Independence Day is Caesar's Birthday July=Julie=Julius,Labor Day is Murderer Day Rituals Death, Columbus Day is a toast too Christopher Columbus wickedness and deceivers in America History which he never discover America.Halloween Day is some Turkish Celtics Greek person wearings some Leprechaun customs and performing rituals and also one of the most wickedness holiday ever because death,witchcraft, and ritual holiday on this pagan ritual day, Veteran Day was added like I said a few minutes ago it for veteran is too celebrate they death too get paid even more than the vet dies it sacrifice ritual for The Power That Be, Thanksgiving is The Slaughter Of The So Call Native Indians the reason I said so call The Dark People that discover America wasn't born Indians or Native they made them names up for them and We Give Thanks to YAHWEH THE MOST HIGH everyday not just one day or once a month or on just Sunday. Christmas Eve is another rituals,Christmas and Xmas is Nimrod's Birthday the wickedness holiday you come across when you research it for yourselves and it not THE BEGOTTEN SON birthday because The Winter Solstice is Nimrod wicked day not YAHWEH BEN YAHWEH THE BEGOTTEN SON was born in the spring not winter.

Let's discuss the Holy Days now The Biblical People celebrated The Passover, The Tabernacles, First Fruit, Hanukkah Day, Feast Day,Unleavened Bread, etc. but Satan had Man changes Holy Days to Holiday Days or you can say Hellidays. THE MOST HIGH YAH told us we can eat meats on these Holy Day what HE created accept The First Fruit Day, we ate lamb, brisket, we eat chicken and fish anyway things HE call Clean Food but YAH didn't want us to eat which call Unclean Food which is shrimp,crablegs,ribs,pork,seafood anything out of an pig or an horse is concerned bad foods like Pork Chops,Pork Sausage,Hotdogs,Bolonga etc and you know the average person go say oh we was raised on pork and anything we eat we bless it and THE MOST HIGH will make it clean which you been taught by poor people. Noddles ain't good for you either it nothing but Wax and research that for yourselves. We don't suppose to eat meat everyday, Eat vegetables sometimes and fruit and THE MOST HIGH said we shall eat and drink poison but yet still live that in Mark chapter.

Page 44

Now let's talk about Safe Sex, People at this day and age is Whitewash to believe in holding sex in today's relationship, people on this I don't have to give you sex and I don't feel like it had a lot of people kill or having less friends, If I want to have sex with a woman then is wrong but if the man have sex with another man is okay, vice versa a woman have sex with another woman is okay, or a man or woman have sex with their pets is ok, Well THE MOST HIGH is NOT down with that wickedness plus having anal sex is wicked and the only way you go catch Aids is anal, taking vaccine shots so much,or being homosexual or bi-sexual. Use condoms doesn't necessary mean safe sex. Don't let Man misguide you like that and ladies stop letting other females tell you mumbo jumbo things but if a guy tell you stuff you ready to call the cops on him, you don't believe him, or every guy trying to get your panties the way you think. A Man or Boy are made to have sex with a Woman or Girl but people think it nasty.

Page 45

To give thanks to THE MOST HIGH is too admit you a sinner,pray too HIM that you did wrong, you here, you still go live for HIM, but we have enter date and exit date here, you pray for things you need not what you want so much, you work for the things to pleased THE MOST HIGH YAHWEH, pray to love yourselves, focus on yourselves, but don't love yourself to the point that it just all about you. The average person go think it a opinion book not a fact or factual book,And God spell Dog backward abbreviation of Dogma, O'siris but people go think I'm blasphemy but I'm really not. And THE MOST HIGH'S SON didn't die on a cross HE died on a tree read 3 Acts chapters,Galatians chapter,and 1 Peter chapter I believe. Some told me that HE never died on a cross.

The Days Of The Weeks wasn't a such thing in Biblical Times until it start in Rome and it's the calendars of Caesar like Sunday, Monday, Tuesday,Wednesday,Thursday,Friday,Saturday. Now Sunday is Sun Day, Monday is Moon Day,Tuesday is Tiws Day, Wednesday is Mercury Day, Thursday is Thor Day, Friday is Venus Day, Saturday is Saturn Day. are of Julius Caesar, Now the month of the year like January,February,March,April, May,June,July,August,September,October,November,December, Which January is Janus it was 29 days until Caesar change it too 31 days,February is Februa it was 28 days until Caesar change 29 and every 4 years it 28 days, March is Mars or Martius it 31 days, April is Aprilis it was 30 days,May is Maia is 31 days, June is Junius or Juno it was 29 days until Caesar change it to 30 days,

July is Julius, Julie,Quintilis is really the 4 is Caesar Birthday and it always was 31 days, August is Sexitilis it was 29 days until Caesar change it to 31 days, September is Septembre it was 29 days until Caesar change it to 30 days, October is Octobre it was always 31 days, November is Novembris it 29 days until Caesar change it to 30 days, December is Decembre first it had 30 days then it was 29 days until Caesar change it to 31 days. The name of the so call planets like Mars,Earth,Mercury,Jupiter,Saturn,Venus,Neptune,Uranus,Sun,Moon,Pluto, Asteroid,Ceres,Gas Giant, Calitso 360 is made up by Caesar because nobody including Lucifer knows the name of the planets that THE MOST HIGH created but it too deep for you so I'm go keep it simple and research the real truth behind it! So the days of the week and months of the year are Roman Mythology and The Gregorian Calendar is Roman Calendars Too. This go be a debate!

Don't thank it just a Black Book it's an reality book for Black People and
others too read and dig deep and don't read it understand it and learn from it
I know people living the fantasy world and living the dream and more lost than
woke. But it isn't to wake the whole world up but is too read and learn. Take it for what
it worth. It for all races of people to read and stay focus don't react before thinking. Think
before react, action speaks louder than words. It not a teach hate type of book don't
be bend out of shape. So it is what it is book! All Praise And Glory THE MOST HIGH.
That's All!

Page 49

Conclusion

My first book ever and it may be long overdue but necessary and let me know what you think.

The End

www.ingramcontent.com/pod-product-compliance
Ingram Content Group UK Ltd.
Pitfield, Milton Keynes, MK11 3LW, UK
UKHW041835200726
13854UKWH00003BA/1144

9 780359 981878